OLD LEEDS

in photographs

VOLUME 2

selected by Brian and Dorothy Payne

Published by Leeds Civic Trust, Claremont, 23 Clarendon Road, Leeds, LS2 9NZ, Yorkshire.

Printed by Fretwell & Cox Limited, Goulbourne Street, Keighley, West Yorkshire, BD21 1PZ.

Introduction

The volume of photographs of Old Leeds being almost out of print, we were given the opportunity to produce another selection. In doing so we realised once again how difficult it is to get away from Briggate, the Headrow and Boar Lane. We were lucky enough to find some of Albion Street, Commercial Street and Vicar Lane.

Where possible we have tried to use good reproductions but in some instances photographs of poorer quality have been used because of their interest. It gets more difficult to select photographs as time goes by, as so many are published because of the increasing interest in local history. We were fortunate to be able to use the photographs of Alan Cockroft, a well known photographer in Horsforth, who kindly offered us the use of his collection and who reproduced many of the prints for us. We would like to thank him for all his help.

Once more we are grateful to the Thoresby Society, and we find that being a member of that society is a great asset to any local historian. The Victorian pamphlets and guide books in the Society's library, are invaluable when identifying photographs. We would also like to thank the Leeds Civic Trust for giving us the opportunity to produce another volume and are pleased to be able to use many of their photographs in this volume.

Photographs used:

L.C.T.   1, 2, 4, 5, 6, 7, 8, 9, 10, 11, 12, 15, 16, 22, 23, 24, 25, 31, 32, 33, 36, 38, 39, 40, 42, 43.

T.S.   3, 13, 26, 27, 28, 41, 44, 49, 50, 51.

A.C.   14, 20, 21, 29, 30, 34, 35, 37, 45, 46, 47, 48, 52, 53, 54, 55, 56, 57, 58.

BAP.   17, 18, 19.

Brian and Dorothy Payne.

1.   Formal opening of City Square, September 16th, 1903.

2. Inside the Leadenhall Carcass Market, Vicar Lane. In 1879 the Leeds regulations for slaughter houses required that they be well flagged, sewered and ventilated. This building was superseded by a new abattoir on a different site in 1899. When it was demolished the site was cleared for the County Arcade development.

3.   A view looking down Cheapside from Briggate towards Vicar Lane. The Cheapside Shambles on the left. Circa 1893.

4.   Vicar Lane showing the entrance to the slaughter house through the arch on the right. It was known as the Leadenhall Carcass Market.

5.   Looking down Briggate where the much narrower Upperhead Row crossed. Edwin Hicks and Co. Drapers occupy the corner shop on Upperhead Row, Hope Brothers and Thornton's arcade further down. The boy on the left has just emptied his bucket down the drain and is trapped in time for us all to see.

6.   The junction of Boar Lane and Briggate with the Trevelyan Temperance Hotel built for Barron the clothier in 1870, when Boar Lane was re-built and widened. The architect was Thomas Ambler. Photograph circa 1900.

7.   Leeds Bridge, built of iron with a single span of 102′–6″. It was designed by T. D. Steele of Newport, Monmouthshire in 1872. This picture is later than we would normally choose but it is too good to leave out. Living in Leeds it is easy to forget the river exists, especially if you live in the North side. Many people never see the river Aire. The picture is taken from the west, the date is uncertain, but the last trams ran in Leeds in the early sixties.

8.   Bridge End and the approach to Leeds Bridge from the corner of Dock Street, these buildings appear to be ready for demolition. The building with the bay windows was originally the Seven Stars Inn. The Adelphi Public House is emerging on the right which would give us a date of circa 1900.

9. The old Police Station at the corner of Woodhouse Moor. This building stood at the junction of Reservoir Street and Woodhouse Lane, the high wall of the reservoir can be seen behind the building, Clarendon Road now starts here. This station was replaced by another police station and Public Library (the two were often built together in Leeds). The later building is still in use by the Leeds Council for Voluntary Service.

10. Hyde Park Corner, looking down Woodhouse Street, the original Hyde Park Hotel on the left. The buildings on the right were replaced and the road widened, cirça 1906.

11. Old buildings at Hyde Park Corner, taken looking down Hyde Park Road from Headingley Lane. Circa 1906.

12. A later view of Hyde Park Corner, looking towards Woodhouse Moor. The old buildings have been replaced by the row of shops in the distance, but it is interesting to note that the block turning the corner into Woodhouse Lane is not yet built. Circa 1911.

13. High density living in Linsley Fold, Mabgate. An intersting collection of old houses, probably about to be demolished. The photograph is dated 16/7/1899.

14. Entrance to Greens Court Lands Lane.

15. Eye Bright Place. A better class of housing with the addition of shops. The photograph is taken at the end of Wellington St., opposite the old Midland Station. It must be later than 1896 as the General Post Office can be seen behind the houses.

16. Entrance to Waterloo Court; Quarry Hill, quite a rabbit warren of buildings with cellar dwellings inside.

17.　"Arncliffe" Shire Oak Road, Headingley, built in 1895 for J. E. Bedford, chemical manufacturer of Leeds. The architect was Frances W. Bedford, of Leeds.

18. The entrance hall at Arncliffe. These pictures are taken from the sale catalogue of 1933.

19. The dining room at Arncliffe, an interesting comparison between this beautiful house, and the type of housing in Linsley Fold and Waterloo Court.

20.   Commercial Street probably at the same time as No. 21. This is taken at the junction of Lands Lane. These buildings
still survive.

21. A busy street scene in Commercial Street, circa 1900.

22. Woodhouse Ridge attracted numerous crowds, the deep slopes dotted with gorse and hawthorn and other areas were laid out with gardens. Band performances were given during the summer. It was one of the attractions offered by the Leeds Tramways, all the way from New Market Street to Meanwood for 2d.

23. In 1897 the Leeds Corporation's own electrically equipped tram route between Kirkstall and Roundhay was opened for traffic, and the public were able to get out to the open spaces with ease. In Burrow's Guide to Leeds 1914, 26 parks and open spaces were listed. These ranged from Woodhouse Moor purchased in 1857, containing over 60 acres, to the small area in Beckett Street of just over 2 acres, purchased in 1905. Most of the parks were provided with bandstands, and during the summer band performances were given on evenings during the week and at holiday times.

24.   Another leisure activity was the walk over Adel Moor to Verity's tea rooms, this was a regular outing for Edwardian families. The house on the left was Mill Fall Cottage, where the Veritys lived. Tea was served to the right of the house and could be eaten in a barn-like structure at the back. This custom was still popular in the 1950s.

25.   Listening to the band in Roundhay Park. The park consisting of 648 acres was purchased by Leeds Corporation in 1872, and was opened the same year by the Duke of Connaught.

26.   North Isle of Kirkstall Abbey before restoration, with Edwardian lady in romantic setting.

27.   Kirkstall Abbey from the south east before restoration. One might be excused for believing that it looks far more interesting than in the next photograph.

28.   The Abbey soon after restoration. Kirkstall Abbey was purchased from the Cardigan family, after the death of the earl in 1888 it was sold by auction to Colonel J. T. North, who afterwards presented it to the City of Leeds. This was in 1889. Colonel North was a Leeds engineer who had made a fortune out of nitrates. A report on the preservation of the ruins was produced by Mr W. H. St. John Hope of the Society of Antiquaries in 1890, but it was not until 1895 that the restoration was completed.

29.   Albion Street looking north.

30.   View of Albion Street with Albion Place on the right. Albion Street was started in 1790 and was intended to be a residential street, but by 1792 a music hall had been erected.

31, 32.   View down Bond Street from the bottom of East Parade, Infirmary Street to the right. The curved tram lines running towards St. Paul's Street, where trams used to run from City Square through Infirmary Street, St. Paul's Street and West Street to join the route to Kirkstall.

33. Corner of Albion Street and Bond Street, the opening off Albion Street leads to the Yorkshire Post office yard. The adjoining premises were re-built by the Yorkshire Post in 1886. The bank building had become Pearce and Sons jewellers by 1914. The Yorkshire Post newspapers remained on this site until the building was demolished, when they transferred to Wellington Street.

34. The junction of Albion Street and Guildford Street (now the Headrow).

35.   The Parish Church, Kirkgate. St. Peter's was re-built on the site of the Medieval Parish Church in 1841, the architect being R. F. Chantrell.

36. Kirkgate north side, buildings directly opposite the Parish Church with the entrance to the graveyard on the right. To the left the entrance to Cherry Tree Yard, the building extreme left is the Old Nags Head.

37. Through the mean narrow opening into the squalor of Cherry Tree Yard.

38. South side of Kirkgate, circa 1910, corner of Wharf Street, the building on the left just beyond the lamp post was the Old Crown Inn, birthplace of the Ancient Order of Foresters, established 1790. Entry to the Old Crown yard was to the left of the doorway. The building was demolished in 1935.

39. Gt. George Street opposite the back of the Town Hall with the Victoria Commercial Hotel on the left, now the popular Victoria public house. The building next door to it was designed by George Corson in 1865 for the photographer E. Wormald for his house and studio. The building still survives but the ground floor facade has gone. The building to the right was the old Masonic Hall built in 1866 by Perkin and sons.

40. The last Medieval frontage in Briggate now demolished, if we can believe the date over the front the building is 1513. On the left the Pack Horse Inn yard.

41.   North side of West Bar, where Boar Lane enters City Square. The premises of Hargreaves and Nussey, Woollen Manufacturers, at the corner of Basinghall Street. The whole is now occupied by the Bond Street Centre. The building just appearing on the left was the Commercial Building demolished in 1871. Note the gentlemen in their stove pipe hats.

42.   The Philosophical Hall, corner of Park row and Bond Street, it became the City Museum later, and it was bombed during the last war. The building was erected in 1819 and enlarged in 1861.

43.   Park Row and the old Post Office, with the railings of the Mixed
Cloth Hall on the left. The statue of Sir Robert Peel, sculptured by
Behnes was placed here in 1852. It was the first statue to be erected in
the streets of Leeds. The statue was moved to the square outside the
Town Hall in 1903 when City Square was formed. It was moved again
in 1937 to Woodhouse Moor.

44. Old Post Office Building, Park row, originally built as the Court House in 1813 and enlarged in 1844. It was purchased for use as the Post Office in 1861, the third storey being added in 1872 for the Postal telegraph.

45. The General Post Office built in 1896 to replace the old building in Park Row. It was on the site of the Mixed Cloth Hall.

46.   Corner of Boar Lane circa 1868. The building at the L.H. side was demolished for street widening. The buildings on the right survived until quite recently. Boar Lane was widened on the left because of Holy Trinity Church being so close to the pavement. Bissingtons hat shop shown here was occupying the same premises in 1853.

47.   Boar Lane after re-building, looking towards Briggate.

48.   Market Buildings Vicar Lane, the markets were originally held in Briggate, they were moved to Vicar Lane in 1823 and became the Kirkgate General Market. A market hall was erected in 1854, this was demolished in 1902 and the present building was opened in 1904. The architects Leeming and Leeming of Halifax were engaged.

49.   Vicar Lane in 1891, on the left the earlier Market building demolished when the present Market was erected. The Greyhound Hotel was originally the House of Recovery.

50. Vicar Lane looking towards the Headrow, the House of Recovery building, now the Greyhound Hotel on the far left. Circa 1890.

51. Vicar Lane before widening and rebuilding, circa 1890.

52. Briggate with cars taking pride of place, circa 1900.

53. Briggate yet again! The street is always full of people, just like today. This is an interesting picture because of the variations in transport. Circa 1910.

54.   The Corner of City Square. This photograph was too good to miss, the entry to Boar Lane with the Royal Exchange
Building on the left, circa 1910.

55.   City Square showing the War Memorial, which was placed here in 1922. It was moved to the garden of rest in 1937 and the angel was taken to Cottingley in 1937. On the right is the original Queens Hotel.

56.   An elaborate Vicar Lane after the great rebuilding of the 1900s.

57. Burley Village near Leeds, looking across to the Victorian development. The only thing that remains now is the village street name.

Old Burley Village

58.   Burley Road looking towards Leeds, circa 1900.